# Easy HTML - Handy Guide

Discover the World of Web Programming

# INDEX

**Links and Anchors**

**Images and Multimedia**

**Table**

**Form e Input**

**Layout and Styling with CSS**

**Security and Best Practices**

**Conclusions and insights**

**Outro**

# Intro

Welcome to the exciting and inspiring journey of "Easy HTML - Handy Guide". This book is a shining beacon that will lead you through the vast and fascinating world of HTML, from basic to deep, with an irresistible energy. You will be transported from the foundations of the language, sinking the roots in the fertile soil of its code, and then ascending the robust trunk of its powerful functions.

Whether you are a beginner hungry for knowledge or an aspiring expert looking for a new challenge, you will not be disappointed. Each chapter will take you to the next level of understanding, with comprehensive explanations and numerous practical examples that will give you the confidence to experiment and create with confidence.

From basic tags to complex structures, you'll learn how to shape the content of your pages with extraordinary craftsmanship. Words will come alive with the formatting of your text, while images will dance between the lines of your code. The links will intertwine, opening doors to new and exciting digital worlds.

But we won't stop there. Through advanced insights, we'll take you to the pinnacle of HTML's power. You'll discover how to handle intricate tables, create interactive forms, and implement stunning layouts with the help of CSS. Your creativity will know no bounds as we guide you through the latest trends and best practices to ensure optimal performance and foolproof security.

Let this book become your reliable compass in the vast ocean of HTML, an indispensable companion for those wishing to master the foundations of digital interaction. Be ready to transform the way you think and create as you discover the power of HTML like never before.

Take control of the web and let the adventure begin!

# Development Environment

## Introduction

This guide includes a dedicated development environment, which means it avoids the need to set up a local development environment, which may vary from computer to computer. Using the included development environment is more convenient and faster, as no software installation is required. In addition, it will be possible to test written pages directly from the browser.

## Configuration

To access the dedicated development environment, log on to https://easy-code.cloud/board . After registering or logging in, you will immediately find the work environment ready to use.

To create a new page click on the 'add' button in the left side column. Enter a name for the page respecting the constraints, choose the desired language via the drop-down menu and finally press 'Create'. You will find a summary of all the pages you have created in the left side column.

To write on a page click on its name: the text editor will open, allowing you to write code on it.

# Introduction to HTML

## What is HTML?

HTML, short for HyperText Markup Language, is a **markup** language used to define the structure and content of web pages. Its main goal is to organize and present information in a consistent and structured manner, making it possible for web pages to be viewed and interacted with by browsers.

HTML is based on a key concept: hypertext. Hypertext is a form of text that contains links (or hyperlinks) that allow users to navigate from one page to another or access different resources within a page. These links, generally represented as underlined text or buttons, allow users to explore the content of Web pages in a nonlinear fashion.

The HTML language uses a series of elements, called tags, to define the structure and meaning of the content within a web page. Each tag is identified by a name enclosed in angle brackets (< >). For example, the <p> tag is used to indicate a paragraph, while the <h1> tag indicates a top-level header.

In addition to the basic tags, HTML offers a wide range of tags that allow you to structure and format text, insert images, create lists, tables, forms, and more. These tags can be nested within one another to create a hierarchical structure that organizes content in a logical manner.

An important aspect of HTML is its neutral nature with respect to the visual appearance of Web pages. HTML focuses on the structure and meaning of the content, while style and appearance are handled through CSS (Cascading Style Sheets). This separation of structure and presentation allows for greater flexibility in web page design and makes it easier to maintain and update the site over time.

In addition, HTML also supports the inclusion of interactive scripts through JavaScript. This allows dynamic features to be added to web pages, such as form validation, event handling, and real-time content updating.

HTML is an open standard and is maintained and developed by a consortium called the World Wide Web Consortium (W3C). The W3C works to ensure that HTML remains a language that is flexible, accessible and interoperable with different browsers and devices.

## The structure of a HTML document

An HTML document is organized in a tree structure, where elements are nested within other elements, forming a hierarchy. The main element of any HTML page is the <html> tag, within which are the <head> tag and the <body> tag. The <head> tag contains header information such as the title of the page, links to CSS stylesheets, and other metadata, while the <body> tag contains the visible content of the page, such as text, images, links, tables, and forms.

Within the <body> tag, a variety of HTML tags can be used to define the structure of the content. For example, the <h1> tag indicates a top-level heading, while <p> tags are used to create paragraphs of text. You can also use tags like <div> and <span> to group and format specific sections of your content.

HTML tags can be nested within each other to create a hierarchical structure. For example, a paragraph can be placed inside a div and the div in turn can be included in another section or container.

Additionally, attributes within HTML tags can be used to provide additional information or define specific behaviors. For example, the "src" attribute is used in the <img> tag to specify the path to the image to display.

# Tags and Basic Elements

## Tags and elements

An HTML "tag" is a keyword enclosed in angle brackets, such as <p>, <h1>, <img>. Tags define the basic elements used to structure and format the content of a web page.

HTML "elements", on the other hand, consist of a combination of HTML tags, their content and associated attributes. For example, consider the following element:

```
<p class="intro">This is an example paragraph.</p>
```

In this case, the element is the opening <p> tag, the text "This is an example paragraph." as its content, and the class="intro" attribute which provides additional information about the element's style or functionality.

Attributes, as in the case of the example above, provide additional information about HTML elements. They can be used to specify styles, identify elements with classes or IDs, provide hyperlinks, and more.

Some common examples of HTML tags include:

-   **<h1>** - **<h6>**: Headings of different levels, where <h1> is the highest in the hierarchy.

-   **<p>**: Text paragraphs.

-   **<a>**: Hyperlinks (links) pointing to other pages or resources.

-   **<img>**: Images to display on the page.

-   **<ul>** and **<that>**: Elements for creating bulleted or numbered lists.

-   **<table>**, **<tr>**, **<td>**: Elements for creating tables and defining table rows and cells.

These are just a few examples, but HTML offers a wide range of tags that allow you to define the structure and content of a web page in a more detailed and specific way.

In summary, HTML tags are keywords enclosed in angle brackets and define the basic elements, while HTML elements consist of the tags, their content and associated attributes. HTML elements are used to structure and format the content of a web page.

## Opening and closing tags

HTML, the use of opening and closing tags is essential to define the structure of the document and indicate where a given element begins and ends.

An HTML opening tag consists of the element name enclosed in angle brackets < >. For example, the opening tag for a paragraph is <p>. This tells the browser that subsequent text will be considered a paragraph.

An HTML closing tag is similar to an opening tag, but also includes a slash "/" immediately following the less than sign <. For example, the closing tag for a paragraph is </p>. This tells the browser that the paragraph is finished.

Here's an example of using the opening and closing tags correctly for a paragraph:

```
<p>This is a paragraph.</p>
```

In the example above, the opening <p> tag indicates the beginning of the paragraph, while the closing </p> tag indicates the end of the paragraph.

It's important to note that some HTML elements, known as "empty elements" or "self-closing elements," don't require a separate closing tag. These elements are used to insert special content, such as images or horizontal lines, and can be written as a single tag.

For example, the <img> element is used to insert an image and does not require a separate closing tag. It can be written as:

```
<img src="image.jpg" alt="Image description">
```

In some cases, you can also shorten the opening and closing tags by using a forward slash "/" within the opening tag. For example:

```
<p/>
```

This is equivalent to <p></p>, indicating that the paragraph is empty.

However, it is important to note that many HTML elements still require the explicit use of the corresponding opening and closing tags to ensure proper document structure. Make sure you use the opening and closing tags correctly for each HTML element to avoid formatting errors and ensure proper structure of your web page.

## Attributes

HTML attributes provide additional information about HTML elements. Attributes are specified within the opening tags of elements and affect the behavior or appearance of those elements.

An HTML attribute consists of a name and a value, separated by an equal sign (=) and enclosed in quotation marks (""). The attribute name specifies the type of information you intend to provide, while the attribute value specifies the desired content or configuration for that attribute.

Here's an example of an HTML attribute:

```
<a href="https://www.example.com">Click here</a>
```

In the example above, the attribute is href, which is used to specify the URL address that the link points to. The attribute value is "https://www.example.com", which is the destination URL of the link.

Some common attributes you can use include:

- **class**: is used to assign one or more CSS classes to an element for specific styling or selection purposes.

- **id**: this is used to assign a unique identifier to an element, allowing you to refer to that element specifically via JavaScript or CSS.

- **src**: is used to specify the path of the image or media file to be displayed or played.

- **everything**: used to provide alternative text that is displayed when an image cannot be loaded or when read by a screen reader.

- **width** and **height**: are used to specify the width and height of an image or media element.

- **disabled**: is used to disable an element such as a button or an input field.

- **value**: is used to specify the default value of an input field.

It's important to note that the available attributes may vary depending on the type of HTML element you're using. You can refer to the official HTML documentation to know the supported attributes for each element.

Also remember that you can use multiple attributes within a single element by separating them with a space. For example:

```
<img src="image.jpg" alt="Image description" width="300" height="200">
```

In this case, the <img> element uses the src, alt, width, and height attributes to specify the image to display, the alt text, and the desired size.

HTML Attributes are a powerful way to customize and configure elements of your web page. Make sure you use the appropriate attributes according to your needs to enrich the user experience on your page.

## Special characters and escape characters

In HTML, some characters have special meanings and cannot be used directly within the HTML code. To correctly represent these special characters, "escape characters" must be used.

An escape character begins with an ampersand (&) and ends with a semicolon (;). After the ampersand, a code or entity is inserted that represents the desired character. Here are some examples of common special characters and their escape characters:

- **&lt;** represents the character "<"

- **&gt;** represents the character ">"

- **&amp;** represents the character "&"

- **&quot;** represents the character (")

- **&apos;** represents the character (')

- ** ** represents a not separable space

For example, if you want to include the "<" character in your HTML code, you need to replace it with &lt;. This way, the browser will interpret the code correctly without mistaking it for an opening HTML tag.

Here is an example of using escape characters:

```
<p>This is an example of special characters: &lt;, &gt;, &amp;</p>
```

In the example above, the "<" character is replaced by &lt;, the ">" character is replaced by &gt;, and the "&" character is replaced by &amp;. The result displayed in the browser will be:

```
This is an example of special characters: <, >, &
```

Escape characters are useful when you need to correctly represent special characters within your HTML code without altering its structure and meaning. Make sure you use the proper escape characters whenever you need to insert a special character into your HTML code.

## Comments

HTML comments are used to insert notes or annotations in the HTML code that will not be displayed on the web page viewed by the browser. Comments are useful for documentation purposes, to make code more readable, or to temporarily remove portions of code without completely deleting it.

To insert a comment in HTML, you can use the following syntax:

```
<!-- This is an HTML comment -->
```

Anything between **<!--** and **-->** is considered a comment and will be ignored by the browser when viewing the web page. You can insert any text, including special characters or lines of code, into comments.

Here's an example of using HTML comments:

```
<!-- This is a comment explaining the purpose of a block of code -->
<div class="header">
  <h1>Page title</h1>
  <!-- <p>This paragraph is not visible at the moment</p> -->
</div>
```

In the example above, the comment is used to explain the role of the <div class="header"> code block by providing more information about its purpose. Also, a comment has been inserted to temporarily "hide" the <p> paragraph.

It is important to remember that HTML comments should not contain sensitive or confidential information, as the source code of a web page can be easily viewed by visitors. Comments are intended primarily for development, maintenance, and developer collaboration purposes.

Using HTML comments can make your code more readable and understandable for you and other developers who may be working on the same project.

# Document Structure

## Doctype

**<!DOCTYPE>** is a declaration used at the start of an HTML document to specify the document type and version of HTML used in the document. Defines the set of rules and syntax that the browser must follow to correctly interpret the HTML code.
Correct use of <!DOCTYPE> is important because it determines how the browser renders and affects the document's compatibility with HTML standards.

Here is an example of how to use the <!DOCTYPE> declaration in an HTML5 document:

```
<!DOCTYPE html>
<html>
  <head>
    <title>Document title</title>
    <!-- Other items in document header -->
  </head>
  <body>
    <!-- Document content -->
  </body>
</html>
```

The <!DOCTYPE html> declaration indicates that the document is written in HTML5, the most recent version of the HTML standard. This doctype is short and simple, and is supported by all modern web browsers.

It's important to note that using the correct doctype can affect how your browser interprets HTML code and applies rendering rules. Using the appropriate doctype helps ensure that the document displays correctly and is consistent across different browsers.

## The <html> tag

The <html> tag is one of the fundamental tags in HTML markup and represents the root element of an HTML document. Every HTML document must begin with the <html> tag and end with the closing </html> tag.

The <html> tag contains the entire content of the HTML document, including the header (<head> tag) and the body (<body> tag). It serves as the main container for all HTML code within the document.

Here is an example of the basic structure of an HTML document using the <html> tag:

```
<!DOCTYPE html>
<html>
<head>
  <!-- Metadata, links, scripts and other header elements -->
</head>
```

```
<body>
  <!-- Visible page content, such as text, images, links, etc. -->
</body>
</html>
```

Within the <html> tag, the <head> tag is used to contain the document header, which includes the document title, metadata, external links, and scripts. The <body> tag, on the other hand, contains the visible content of the page, such as text, images, links and other interactive elements.

Using the properly structured <html> tag helps the browser interpret the document correctly and provides an organized basis for the HTML code. It is important to ensure that the HTML document is always enclosed within the <html> tag to ensure correct interpretation by the browser.

## Il tag <head>

The <head> tag is an HTML element that is used to contain the header of the document. It is located inside the <html> tag and precedes the <body> tag. The content within the <head> tag is not displayed directly on the web page, but provides additional information about the HTML document.

Some of the common elements found within the <head> tag include:

**<title>**: The <title> tag is used to specify the title of the document. This title appears in the browser title bar or browser tab when the page is opened. For example:

```
<title>Document Title</title>
```

**<meta>**: The <meta> tag is used to provide metadata about the HTML document, such as the description of the document, keywords associated with the content, the character set used, and other information. Example:

```
<meta name="description" content="Document description">
<meta name="keywords" content="keyword1, keyword2, keyword3">
```

**<link>**: The <link> tag is used to link the HTML document to other external files, such as cascading style sheets, custom fonts or site icons. For example:

```
<link rel="stylesheet" href="style.css">
<link rel="icon" href="favicon.ico">
```

**<script>**: The <script> tag is used to link the document to external JavaScript scripts or to include scripts directly within the header. As an example:

```
<script src="script.js"></script>
```

Other elements such as <style>, <base>, <noscript>, etc., which provide additional functionality and instructions for the browser.

Using the <head> tag is essential to provide important information and configure the HTML document. It contains elements that affect the document's appearance, behavior, and indexing, but are not directly visible to users visiting the page.

## The <body> tag

The <body> tag is an HTML element that contains the visible content of a web page. It is located inside the <html> tag and follows the <head> tag. The content within the <body> tag is displayed directly on the web page and represents what users will see and interact with when they visit the site.

Some examples of elements that can be included within the <body> tag are:

**Text**: You can include plain text using formatting tags such as <h1> for headings, <p> for paragraphs, and <span> for specific pieces of text. For example:

```
<h1>Main Title</h1>
<p>This is a paragraph of text.</p>
<span>This is specific text.</span>
```

**Images**: You can embed images using the <img> tag, specifying the URL of the image and optionally adding attributes such as alt for the textual description of the image.
Example:

```
<img src="image.jpg" alt="Image description">
```

**Link**: You can create links to other web pages using the <a> tag. Specify the destination URL in the href attribute value. Example follows:

```
<a href="https://www.example.com">Visit the example site</a>
```

**Form elements**: You can include HTML forms to collect input from users. For example, <input>, <textarea>, <select> and <button> tags are commonly used to create input fields, text areas, drop-down menus and buttons. For example:

```
<form>
  <label for="name">Name:</label>
  <input type="text" id="nome" name="nome">
  <br>
  <label for="email">Email:</label>
  <input type="email" id="email" name="email">
  <br>
  <button type="submit">Invia</button>
```

```
</form>
```

Other elements such as tables, lists, multimedia elements (audio and video), presentation elements (for example, <div> and <span>), and much more.

The content within the <body> tag forms the main interface of the web page and determines what users see and interact with. This is where the relevant content and HTML markup that defines the structure and presentation of the page is placed.

# Text formatting

## Paragraphs and Blank Lines

In HTML, paragraphs are created using the tag**<p>**. The <p> tag tells the browser that its content represents a paragraph of text. Text inside the <p> tag is usually displayed with white space above and below it.

Here's an example of how to use the <p> tag to create a paragraph:

```
<p>This is an example paragraph.</p>
```

If you want to create more paragraphs, you can simply place more <p> tags in your HTML code:

```
<p>First paragraph.</p>
<p>Second paragraph.</p>
<p>Third paragraph.</p>
```

As for blank lines, you can get blank space between paragraphs or other sections of your HTML document by using a blank line tag or by inserting multiple tags**<br>**.

Here's an example of how to use a blank line tag <br> to get a blank space:

```
<p>First paragraph.</p>
<br>
<p>Second paragraph.</p>
```

Alternatively, you can use a double <br> tag to get a bigger space:

```
<p>First paragraph.</p>
<br><br>
<p>Second paragraph.</p>
```

It is recommended to use <p> tags for regular text paragraphs and <br> tags only for blank lines within a paragraph or in specific situations where you want smaller white space.

## Heading

Headings are used to define the hierarchy of the text and give structure and organization to the page. Headings range from level **h1** (most important) to the level **h6** (least important). Heading level indicates the relative size and importance of the text.

Here's an example of how to use HTML headers:

```
<h1>Level 1 entitlement</h1>
<h2>Level 2 certificate</h2>
<h3>Level 3 Intestacy</h3>
<h4>Level 4 Intestacy</h4>
<h5>Level 5 Intestacy</h5>
<h6>Level 6 Intestacy</h6>
```

The <h1> tag represents the top-level header, usually used for the main title of the page. The <h2> tag is used for important subtitles, followed by <h3>, <h4>, <h5>, <h6> for decreasing importance levels.

Text within headings usually appears bold and in a larger font size than normal paragraph text.

It is important to use headings appropriately and consistently to create a logical and accessible structure for your web page. Headings also help search engines understand the organization of page content and can affect your ranking in search results.

## Text in Bold and Italics

you can apply bold text style using tag**<strong>** O**<b>**, while you can apply the italic text style using the tag**<em>** O**<i>**. These tags serve to semantically indicate that the text within them should be bolded or italicized, but the actual appearance may vary depending on the cascading style sheets applied to the document.

Here's an example of how to use bold and italic text tags:

```
<p>This is <strong>bold text</strong>.</p>
<p>This is <b>bold text</b>.</p>

<p>This is <em>italicized</em> text.</p>
<p>This is <i>italicized</i> text.</p>
```

Both <strong> and <b> tags are used to denote bold text, and there is no significant semantic difference between them. However, for best practice reasons, it is recommended to use <strong> when text has strong importance or particular meaning, such as keywords or important concepts within the content.

Similarly, both the <em> and <i> tags are used to indicate italicized text. Again, there are no significant semantic differences between them. However, it is recommended to use <em> when text has particular importance or emphasis, such as quotations or words in a different context from the surrounding text.

## Underline and Strikethrough

You can apply the underline text style using the tag**<u>**, while you can apply the strikethrough text style using the tag**<s>**, **<strike>** O**<of>**. These tags serve to semantically indicate that the text within them should be underlined or crossed out, but the actual appearance may vary depending on the CSS style sheets applied to the document.

Here's an example of how to use tags for underlined and strikethrough text:

```
<p>This is <u>underlined</u> text.</p>

<p>This is <s>strikeout</s> text.</p>
<p>This is <strike>strikeout</strike> text.</p>
<p>This is <del>strikeout</del> text.</p>
```

The <u> tag is used to indicate underlined text. However, excessive use of underlining can lead to confusion as it is commonly associated with hyperlinks. Therefore, it is generally recommended to use the underlined text style only to indicate particular emphasis or meaning.

For strikethrough text, you can use one of the following tags: <s>, <strike>, <del>. All of these tags are accepted and interpreted by user agents, but <s> and <strike> are deprecated under the HTML5 specification, so it is recommended to use <del> to indicate strikethrough text.


## Citations and References

You can use the tag**<blockquote>** to indicate a quotation or text excerpt that comes from another source. This tag is often used to quote other people's text or to highlight a relevant block of text in the context of the web page.

Here is an example of how to use the <blockquote> tag:

```
<blockquote>
  <p>Wisdom is the best thing a man could wish for.</p>
  <cite>Plato</cite>
</blockquote>
```

In the example above, the <blockquote> tag outlines the block of text representing the quote. The <p> tag within the <blockquote> tag is used to hold the actual text of the quote. You can format text within <blockquote> using other HTML tags such as paragraphs, lists, or other formatting elements.

You can also include a tag **<cite>** within the <blockquote> tag to indicate the author or source of the quote. The <cite> tag is used to highlight the reference to the source of the cited text.

In addition to the <blockquote> tag, you can use the tag **<q>** for short quotes within a paragraph. The <q> tag indicates that the text within it is a quote and can be rendered appropriately by user agents.

Here is an example of how to use the <q> tag:

```
<p>The pain itself is important, it will be followed by the education system. <q>Carpe diem</q>, said the poet.</p>
```

In the example above, the text "Carpe diem" is treated as a quote within the paragraph.

## Ordered and Unordered Lists

You can create ordered and unordered lists using tags respectively **<ol>** and **<ul>**. Ordered lists are numbered lists, while unordered lists are bulleted lists.

**Ordered list**:

```
<ol>
 <li>First element</li>
 <li>Second element</li>
 <li>Third element</li>
</ol>
```

The sorted list is created using the <ol> tag, and each element of the list is defined within the <li> tag. The browser will automatically show the numbers or dots for each item in the sorted list.

**Unordered list**:

```
<ul>
 <li>First element</li>
 <li>Second element</li>
 <li>Third element</li>
</ul>
```

The unordered list is created using the <ul> tag, and each element of the list is defined within the <li> tag. The browser will automatically show the points for each item in the unordered list.

You can also create nested lists, i.e. lists within other lists, to create a hierarchical structure. Just insert a new <ul> or <ol> tag and the related <li> inside a <li> element of another list.

Here is an example of a nested list:

```
<ul>
 <li>First element
  <ul>
   <li>Subelement 1</li>
   <li>Subelement 2</li>
  </ul>
 </li>
 <li>Second element</li>
</ul>
```

In the example above, an unordered list with two elements is created. The first element has a list nested within it, with two sub-elements.

# Links and Anchors

## Creating Hypertext Links

HTML offers a powerful tool for creating hyperlinks, allowing users to navigate between different web pages, access external resources, and create links between content. Hyperlinks are one of the fundamental pillars of the modern web and play a crucial role in users' navigation and interaction with websites.

Creating a hyperlink in HTML is a simple but important process. To do that, you need to use the tag**<a>**, which stands for "anchor" or "link". This tag is used as a container for clickable text or images that serve as a starting point for the link.

To specify the destination of the link, the href attribute must be used, which contains the URL of the target resource. This can be an external URL starting with "http://" or "https://", or a relative URL that refers to other pages or resources within your website.

Once the link is created, users can click on it to be redirected to the specified destination. This opens up new browsing possibilities, allowing users to explore related content, access additional resources, or jump to specific pages within a website.

Hyperlinks can be used for multiple purposes such as linking navigation pages, providing references to external sources, creating navigation menus, linking to specific sections within a page, and so much more. Their creation and correct use are essential to ensure a good user experience and intuitive navigation.

## Use of Internal Links (Anchors)

you can use internal links, also known as anchors or "anchors", to link to specific sections within the same webpage. Anchors allow users to quickly scroll to a certain section without having to manually scroll the entire page.

**Define the anchor**:
Within the target section, you must define an anchor using the id attribute. For example:

```
<h2 id="section1">Section 1</h2>
<p>Content of section 1</p>
```

In the example above, we created an anchor named "section1" inside an <h2> element.

**Create the internal link**:
Now you can create the internal link pointing to the anchor. You can do this by using the <a> tag and setting the value of the href attribute to "#<anchor_name>". For example:

```
<a href="#section1">Go to section 1</a>
```

In the example above, we created a link pointing to the "section1" anchor.

When the user clicks on the internal link, the browser will automatically scroll to the corresponding section in the visible area of the page.

It's important to note that the anchor's id attribute must be unique within the page. Make sure you use separate names for each section you want to link with anchors.

You can use internal links to improve navigation within a long web page or to create a "scroll up" navigation in your site's header or menu. Anchors provide a convenient and intuitive navigation experience within the same page.

## External Links and URLs

You can create external links to link to resources outside your current webpage, such as other webpages, images, documents, videos, and more. To create an external link, you must use the <a> tag and href attribute to specify the destination URL.

Here is an example of how to create an external link:

```
<a href="https://www.example.com">Visit Example.com</a>
```

In the example above, the value of the href attribute is set to the destination URL "https://www.example.com". This will be the actual link that the browser will open when the user clicks on the link.

You can also use relative URLs to link to resources within the same website. For example:

```
<a href="/pages/contact.html">Contact us</a>
```

In this case, the destination URL is relative to the current file path. So if the current path is "https://www.example.com/pages/products.html", the link will lead to the page "https://www.example.com/pages/contact.html".

To open the link in a new browser window or tab, you can use the target attribute with the value "_blank". For example:

```
<a href="https://www.example.com" target="_blank">Open in new tab</a>
```

In this case, when the user clicks on the link, the landing page will open in a new browser window or tab.

It is important to ensure that URLs are correct and well-formed to avoid mislinking. Always include the appropriate protocol (such as "http://" or "https://") for external web links.

External links are essential for connecting your website to other resources and allowing users to explore and access external content. Use them appropriately to provide a complete and engaging browsing experience.

## Links to Email Addresses

You can also create direct links to email addresses, allowing users to automatically open their default email client with a new, pre-addressed email message.

To link to an email address, use the <a> tag and href attribute, followed by mailto: and the desired email address.

Here's an example of how to create a link to an email address:

```
<a href="mailto:example@email.com">Email us</a>
```

In the example above, we used the href attribute with the value "mailto:example@email.com". When the user clicks on the link, their device's default email client will open with a new email addressed to the specified address.

You can also customize the link text however you want, for example:

```
<a href="mailto:example@email.com">Send an email</a>
```

In this case, the link text appears as "Send an email," but remains linked to the specified email address.

Email address links are especially useful when you want to encourage users to contact you directly via email. Make sure you enter a valid and working email address to ensure messages can be delivered correctly.

By using email address links, you can streamline the contact process for your website users and facilitate direct email communication.

## Links to Multimedia Files

You can create links to multimedia files such as images, videos, audios or downloadable documents. This allows you to provide your users with access to additional content or offer to download specific files.

To link to a media file, use the <a> tag and href attribute, specifying the path to the file as the value of the href attribute.

Link to an **image**:

```
<a href="path/to/image.jpg">Show image</a>
```

In this case, the link points to an image called "image.jpg" in the specified path.

Link to a **video**:

```
<a href="path/to/video.mp4">Watch the video</a>
```

In this example, the link points to a video file called "video.mp4" in the specified path.

Link to a **file audio**:

```
<a href="path/to/audio.mp3">Hear the audio</a>
```

The above link points to an audio file called "audio.mp3" in the specified path.

Link to a **downloadable document**:

```
<a href="path/to/document.pdf" download>Download the document</a>
```

By adding the download attribute, the browser will start downloading the file instead of viewing it directly.

Make sure you specify the correct path to the media file in the href attribute value. You can use relative or absolute paths depending on the location of the file relative to the current HTML page.

By creating links to media files, you give users the ability to view, listen to, or download the content they want. Make sure your files are accessible and supported formats are compatible with your users' browsers and devices.

# Images and Multimedia

## Inserting Images

Images are a fundamental visual element to enrich the content of a web page and capture the attention of users.

To insert an image into an HTML page, we use the tag**<img>**. This tag requires no attributes, but does need the src value, which specifies the path to the desired image.

Here is an example of how to insert an image:

```
<img src="path/image.jpg">
```

In the example above, we used the src attribute to specify the path to the desired image. The path can be an absolute URL pointing to the image on the internet or a relative path pointing to the image within your website.

It is important to note that without any additional attributes, the image will display at its original size.

## Image Attributes

When working with images in HTML, you can use various attributes to customize their behavior and appearance. Here is an overview of some common attributes that can be used with the <img> tag:

- **src**: This attribute specifies the path to the image. Must be a URL pointing to the desired image. For example: src="path/image.jpg".

- **everything**: This attribute provides an alternative description of the image. Shown when the image cannot be loaded or for visually impaired users using assistive technologies. For example: alt="Image description".

- **width**: This attribute specifies the width of the image in pixels. For example: width="300".

- **height**: This attribute specifies the height of the image in pixels. For example: height="200".

- **title**: This attribute provides a description text that appears when the user hovers over the image. For example: title="Title of the image".

- **loading**: This attribute specifies the image loading behavior. Possible values include "eager" for immediate loading, "lazy" for delayed loading, and "auto" for default browser behavior. For example: loading="lazy".

- **decoding**: This attribute specifies how the browser decodes the image. Possible values include "async" for an asynchronous decoder, "sync" for a synchronous decoder, and "auto" for a default browser behavior. For example: decoding="async".

Here's a practical example that illustrates the use of image attributes:

```
<img src="path/to/image.jpg" alt="Image description" width="300" height="200" title="Titolo dell'immagine"
loading="lazy">
```

## Image Formats Supported

In HTML, there are several image formats supported by modern browsers. Here is a list of the most common image formats used in HTML:

- **JPEG** (Joint Photographic Experts Group): This format is best for complex photographic images, such as photos taken with a camera. It offers good image quality with data compression that reduces file size. You can use the .jpg or .jpeg extension to denote a JPEG file.

- **PNG** (Portable Network Graphics): This format is suitable for images with areas of solid color or with transparency. Can be used for icons, logos or images with text. It maintains good image quality without any data loss and supports transparency. You can use the .png extension to denote a PNG file.

- **GIF** (Graphics Interchange Format): This format is often used for simple animations or images with few colors. It supports single frame animation and transparency. However, because it uses a limited color palette, it may not be suitable for complex or photographic images. You can use the .gif extension to mean a GIF file.

- **SVG** (Scalable Vector Graphics): This vector image format is based on XML and is ideal for scalable graphics. It can be resized without loss of quality and supports editing images via code. You can use the .svg extension to denote an SVG file.

It is important to choose the most suitable image format based on the type of image and the needs of your website. Consider image quality, file size, and browser support when choosing your format. Also remember to optimize your images for the web to reduce file sizes and improve page load times.

## Audio e Video HTML5

HTML5 introduced built-in support for playing audio and video directly in the browser, without the need for external plugins. You can use items **<audio>** and **<video>** to insert and play audio and video files within your HTML pages.

Here's how you can use the <audio> element to insert an audio file:

```
<audio src="path/audio.mp3" controls>
  Your browser does not support the audio element.
</audio>
```

In the example above, we used the src attribute to specify the path to the audio file we wish to play. The attribute **controls** adds a standard control interface for audio playback, including buttons for play, pause and volume adjustment. If the browser does not support the specified audio element or format, the fallback message "Your browser does not support the audio element."

Similarly, you can use the <video> element to insert a video file:

```
<video src="path/video.mp4" controls>
  Your browser does not support the video element.
</video>
```

Again, the src attribute specifies the path to the video file to play and the controls attribute adds the standard playback controls.

Besides the src and controls attribute, there are other attributes you can use to customize audio and video playback. Some examples include:

- **autoplay**: Start playback automatically when the page is loaded.

- **loop**: Play the file in continuous loop.

- **muted**: Set the volume to mute.

- **poster**: Specifies a preview image to show before playing the video.

- **preload**: Specifies how the browser should load media data. Possible values include "auto" for an automatic load, "metadata" to load metadata only, and "none" to load nothing beforehand.

# Table

## Creating Tables

Tables are a building block of HTML that allow you to organize and display data in a tabular structure. Tables are made up of rows and columns, where the rows represent the data items and the columns represent the different properties or attributes of those items.

Tables are widely used to represent tabular data such as lists, calendars, search results, schedules, and so much more. They can provide an orderly and structured view of the data, making it easier for users to understand and interpret the information.

To create a table in HTML, you can use the element **<table>**, which acts as a container for all rows and columns in the table. Here is a basic syntax for creating a table:

```
<table>
 <tr>
  <td>Data 1</td>
  <td>Data 2</td>
  <td>Data 3</td>
 </tr>
 <tr>
  <td>Data 4</td>
  <td>Data 5</td>
  <td>Data 6</td>
 </tr>
</table>
```

In the example above, we used the <table> element to create a table. Within the table, we have used the <tr> element to define the rows of the table.

Table cells are represented by the <td> element, which contains the actual cell data. We entered the data into the cells of the next rows after the column headers.

Additional rows and columns can be added to the table using the <tr> element and the <td> element in a similar way.

## Table structure

Here is an overview of the table structure in HTML:

- Element **<table>**: The <table> element is the main container of the table and encloses all the other elements of the table.

- Element **<tr>**: The <tr> element defines a row of the table. It is placed inside the <table> element. Each row of the table must be enclosed within a <tr> element.

- Element **<td>**: The <td> element is used to define a table cell. Each cell must be placed inside a <tr> element. Cells can contain text, images, links or other elements.

Below is an example of the basic structure of an HTML table with two rows and three columns.

```
<table>
 <tr>
  <td>Data 1</td>
  <td>Data 2</td>
  <td>Data 3</td>
 </tr>
 <tr>
  <td>Data 4</td>
  <td>Data 5</td>
  <td>Data 6</td>
 </tr>
</table>
```

In the example above, we have a <table> element enclosing two <tr> lines. Both rows contain <td> cells.

It's important to remember that a table can have any number of rows and columns depending on your needs. You can add additional rows using multiple <tr> elements within the <table> element, and you can add more cells in each row using <td> elements.

## Column and Row headers

You can use items **<th>** to define column and row headers in tables. Column headers are typically placed in the first row of the table, while row headers are placed in the first column of the table.

Here's an example of using <th> elements to create column and row headers:

```
<table>
 <tr>
  <th></th>
  <th>Column 1</th>
  <th>Column 2</th>
  <th>Column 3</th>
 </tr>
 <tr>
  <th>Row 1</th>
  <td>Data 1</td>
  <td>Data 2</td>
  <td>Data 3</td>
 </tr>
 <tr>
  <th>Row 2</th>
```

```
    <td>Data 4</td>
    <td>Data 5</td>
    <td>Data 6</td>
  </tr>
</table>
```

In the example above, we used the <th> element to create the column and row headers. The <th> element is similar to the <td> element, but is used specifically for headers.
In the first row of the table, we placed <th> elements to create the column headers. The empty header (<th></th>) in the first column creates an empty space in the upper left of the table.
In the following lines, we used the <th> element to create the line headers. These row headers are placed in the first column of each row.

Column and row headers can contain text or other HTML elements such as links, images or form elements.

Using column and row headings in tables is important for improving the accessibility and understanding of your data. It helps users to easily identify information in different table columns and rows.


## Union of Cells

In HTML tables, you can merge cells horizontally or vertically to create a more complex structure. This can be useful when you want to combine adjacent cells to create wider columns or rows.

To merge cells horizontally the attribute used is **colspan**, while the attribute used to merge cells vertically is **rowspan**. Here's how you can use these attributes:

**Merging Cells Horizontally (colspan)**

```
<table>
  <tr>
   <th colspan="2">Heading Columns 1 and 2</th>
   <th>Heading Column 3</th>
  </tr>
  <tr>
   <td>Data 1</td>
   <td>Data 2</td>
   <td>Data 3</td>
  </tr>
</table>
```

In the example above, we used colspan="2" on the first column header to indicate that it should be merged with the second column. This creates a larger column that encompasses both columns. The third column has no colspan specified, so it remains as a separate column.

**Merging Cells Vertically (rowspan)**

```
<table>
 <tr>
  <th rowspan="2">Column 1 Header</th>
  <th>Column 2 Heading</th>
  <th>Heading Column 3</th>
 </tr>
 <tr>
  <td>Data 1</td>
  <td>Data 2</td>
 </tr>
 <tr>
  <td>Data 3</td>
  <td>Data 4</td>
  <td>Data 5</td>
 </tr>
</table>
```

In the example above, we used rowspan="2" on the first column header to indicate that it should be merged with the second row. This creates a topmost cell that spans both rows. The other columns have no rowspan specified, so they remain as separate cells.

You can combine both horizontal and vertical joining at the same time. For example, you can have a cell that spans multiple rows and columns using both rowspan and colspan.

Be sure to carefully consider table structure and cell merging to maintain a consistent and readable layout.

## Table styling with CSS

HTML tables can be customized and styled using Cascading Style Sheets (CSS) to change the appearance of cells, borders, background and more. You can use various CSS properties to style tables. Here are some common examples of how you can style HTML tables with CSS:

Property **border**: You can use the border property to define cell and table borders. For example:

```
table {
  border-collapse: collapse;
}

th, td {
  border: 1px solid black;
}
```

Property **background-color**: You can use the background-color property to set the background color of cells or rows. For example:

```
th {
  background-color: lightgray;
}

tr:nth-child(even) {
  background-color: #f2f2f2;
}
```

Property **text-align**: You can use the text-align property to align text within cells. For example:

```
th, td {
  text-align: center;
}
```

Property **padding** and **margin**: You can use the padding and margin properties to adjust the internal and external space of cells and tables. For example:

```
table {
  padding: 10px;
}

th, td {
  padding: 5px;
  margin: 2px;
}
```

Property **font-size** and **font-weight**: You can use the font-size and font-weight properties to set the text size and font weight of cells. For example:

```
th {
  font-size: 18px;
  font-weight: bold;
}

td {
  font-size: 14px;
}
```

You can use inline CSS within style attributes of HTML tags to apply specific styles to a single table or element. However, it is recommended to use external CSS, placing the style rules in a separate CSS file and linking it to your HTML document using the <link> element. See the chapter "Layout and Styling with CSS" for further explanations.

# Form e Input

## Introduction to HTML Forms

HTML forms are a powerful tool that allows users to interact with a web page by submitting data to the server. Forms are widely used for creating forms, questionnaires, comment areas, and more. They allow users to enter information such as text, selections, checkboxes, and more, which is then sent to the server for processing.

The basic structure of an HTML form is defined by the element **<form>**, which encloses the input elements and their labels. Here's an example of how you can create a simple HTML form:

```
<form action="/process_form" method="POST">
  <label for="name">Name:</label>
  <input type="text" id="name" name="name" required>

  <label for="email">Email:</label>
  <input type="email" id="email" name="email" required>

  <input type="submit" value="Send">
</form>
```

In the example above, we used the <form> element to create a form. The action attribute specifies the URL or path to the server that will handle the data submitted by the form. The method attribute specifies the method of sending the data to the server, which can be "GET" or "POST".

Within the form, we have used elements **<label>** to create the labels associated with the input elements. The for attribute of the <label> element corresponds to the id attribute of the input element it is associated with.

The elements **<input>** represent the input elements of the form. In our example, we used the type, id, name, and required attributes to create input fields for name and email. The type attribute specifies the type of input (for example, "text" for text, "email" for email), while the required attribute indicates that the field is required.

Finally, the <input> element with the type="submit" attribute creates a submit button that users can click to submit the form to the server.

When the user submits the form, the data is collected and sent to the server for processing. The server can then return a response that can be displayed to users or used to perform other actions.

## Input Fields for Text and Password

You can use <input> elements to create text and password input fields.

**Input field for text**:

```
<label for="name">Name:</label>
```

```
<input type="text" id="name" name="name" placeholder="Enter your name" required>
```

In the example above, we used the <input> element with the attribute **type="text"** to create an input field for text. The id attribute is used to uniquely identify the input field, while the name attribute specifies the name of the field that will be used to identify the value sent to the server. The placeholder attribute specifies sample text that appears in the input field and can provide guidance to users. Finally, the required attribute indicates that the field is mandatory and must be filled in before submitting the form.

**Input field for password**:

```
<label for="password">Password:</label>
<input type="password" id="password" name="password" required>
```

In the example above, we used the <input> element with the attribute **type="password"** to create a password input field. The id attribute is used to identify the input field, while the name attribute specifies the name of the field for sending the data to the server. The required attribute indicates that the field is required and must be filled in.

Remember that password input fields hide the text entered by users, replacing it with dots or asterisks to ensure the safety of sensitive information.

You can further customize these input fields using additional attributes such as maxlength to specify the maximum number of characters allowed, pattern to apply a certain regular expression for data validation, and many more.


## Checkbox and Radio Button

You can use <input> elements to create checkboxes and radio buttons. These elements allow users to select one or more options from a predefined list. Here's how you can use these items:

**Checkbox**:

```
<input type="checkbox" id="option1" name="option1" value="option1">
<label for="option1">Option 1</label>

<input type="checkbox" id="option2" name="option2" value="opzione2">
<label for="option2">Opzione 2</label>
```

In the example above, we used the <input> element with the attribute **type="checkbox"** to create two checkboxes. The id attribute is used to uniquely identify each checkbox, while the name attribute specifies the name of the field for sending the data to the server. The value attribute defines the value associated with each checkbox that will be sent to the server if the checkbox is checked. The <label> element is used to create the label associated with each checkbox using the for attribute which corresponds to the id attribute of the <input> element.

**Radio button**:

```
<input type="radio" id="option1" name="option" value="opzione1">
<label for="option1">Option 1</label>

<input type="radio" id="option2" name="option" value="opzione2">
<label for="option2">Opzione 2</label>
```

In the example above, we used the <input> element with the attribute **type="radio"** to create two radio buttons. Option elements with the same name attribute form an option group in which only one option can be selected. The id attribute is used to uniquely identify each radio button, while the name attribute specifies the name of the field for sending the data to the server. The value attribute defines the value associated with each radio button that will be sent to the server if the option is selected. Again, the <label> element is used to create the label associated with each radio button.

## Dropdown Menu and Multiple Selection

In HTML, you can use elements **<select>** and **<option>** to create a dropdown menu and a multi-select field within your forms. Here's how you can use them:

**Drop down menu**:

To create a dropdown menu, you can use the <select> element and add <option> elements inside it. Each <option> element represents a menu item. Here is an example:

```
<select>
  <option value="option1">Option 1</option>
  <option value="option2">Option 2</option>
  <option value="option3">Option 3</option>
</select>
```

In this example, the user can only select one option from the drop-down menu.

**Multiple selection**:

If you want to allow the user to select multiple options at once, you can add the multiple attribute to the <select> element. Here is an example:

```
<select multiple>
  <option value="option1">Option 1</option>
  <option value="option2">Option 2</option>
  <option value="option3">Option 3</option>
</select>
```

With the multiple attribute, the user can select multiple options by holding down the "Ctrl" key (on Windows) or the "Command" key (on macOS) while clicking on the desired options.

## File selection

In HTML, you can use the <input> element with the attribute **type="file"** to allow the user to select and submit files through a form. Here's how you can use this feature:

```
<form>
 <input type="file" name="fileUpload">
 <input type="submit" value="Upload file">
</form>
```

In the example above, the <input> element of type "file" creates an input field through which the user can select the file to upload. The name attribute specifies the name of the input field, which will be used to identify the file when submitting the form to the server.

Once the user has selected the file, he can submit the form by clicking on the "Upload File" button. When the form is submitted, the file is transmitted to the server along with the other form data for processing.

You can add other attributes to the <input type="file"> element to customize its behavior. For example, the accept attribute can be used to specify accepted file types. Here is an example:

```
<input type="file" name="fileUpload" accept=".jpg, .png, .pdf">
```

In the example above, the input field only accepts files with .jpg, .png and .pdf extensions.

Remember that uploading files via HTML forms requires additional server-side processing and management to save the files to the server or process them in some way, such as using PHP.

## Enter and Reset buttons

you can use <input> elements of type "submit" and "reset" to create submit and reset buttons within your forms. Here's how you can use them:

**Submit button**:

The submit button is used to submit the form data to the server for processing. You can create a submit button using the <input> element with the attribute **type="submit"**. Here is an example:

```
<form>
 <!-- input fields... -->

 <input type="submit" value="Send">
</form>
```

In the example above, when the user clicks the "Submit" button, the form data will be sent to the server for processing.

**Reset button:**

The reset button is used to reset the form field values to their default values. You can create a reset button using the <input> element with the attribute **type="reset"**. Here is an example:

```
<form>
  <!-- input fields... -->

  <input type="reset" value="Reset">
</form>
```

In the example above, when the user clicks the "Reset" button, the values of the form fields will be reset to their default values.


## <input> attributes

The <input> elements in HTML support several attributes that allow you to customize and define the behavior of input fields in forms. Here is a list of common attributes you can use with <input> elements:

- **type**: Specifies the type of input. Some common values include text, password, email, number, checkbox, radio, file, etc.

- **name**: Specifies the name of the input field. It is used to identify the value sent to the server when the form is submitted.

- **value**: Specifies the default value of the input field.

- **placeholder**: Show sample text in the input field when it is empty.

- **required**: Indicates that the input field is mandatory and must be filled in before sending the form.

- **disabled**: Disable the input field, preventing users from interacting with it.

- **readonly**: Make the input field read-only.

- **maxlength**: Specifies the maximum number of characters that can be entered in the input field.

- **min** and **max**: Specify the minimum and maximum value allowed for numeric input fields.

- **step**: Specifies the increment range for numeric input fields.

- **pattern**: Specifies a regular expression that the input field value must match to be valid.

- **autocomplete**: Enable or disable the browser's autocomplete feature for the input field.

- **autofocus**: Automatically set the focus on the input field when the page loads.

- **multiple**: Allows you to select multiple files at once in the file type input field.

- **accept**: Specifies the accepted file types for the file type input field.

- **form**: Specifies which form the input field belongs to.

- **size**: Specifies the visible width of the input field.

These are just some of the more common attributes you can use with <input> elements. You can combine these attributes and use other specific attributes according to your needs.

# Layout and Styling with CSS

## Linking an External Style Sheet

**CSS** (Cascading Style Sheets) is a style sheet language used to define the appearance and formatting of an HTML document. Through CSS, styles such as colors, sizes, fonts, and layouts can be applied to different parts of a web page. External style sheets, linked to HTML documents, allow a clear separation between the structure of the document and its visual presentation, improving the maintainability and flexibility of the code.

To link an external style sheet to an HTML page, you can follow these steps:

Create a separate CSS file with the .css extension which will contain the styling rules for your page. For example, save the file as "style.css".

Inside the HTML document, inside the <head> element, add the <link> element with the necessary attributes. Here is an example:

```
<!DOCTYPE html>
<html>
<head>
  <link rel="stylesheet" href="style.css">
</head>
<body>
  <!-- Page content -->
</body>
</html>
```

In the example above, the href attribute of the <link> element specifies the path to the external CSS file, in this case style.css. Make sure you specify the correct path to your CSS file, taking into account your project's folder structure.

In your external CSS file, you can define styling rules for different parts of the HTML page using CSS selectors. For example, you can select <h1> elements and apply a specific color or font size. Here is an example:

```
h1 {
  color: blue;
  font-size: 24px;
}
```

In the example above, all top-level headers <h1> will be rendered with a blue color and a font size of 24 pixels.

The external style sheet will then be linked to your HTML page and the style rules defined in the CSS file will be applied to the page content.

Using an external style sheet offers the advantage of separating the presentation (styles) from the content (HTML), allowing for better organization and maintenance of the code. Plus, it can be reused across pages, promoting design consistency.

## Inline and Internal Style

In HTML, there are several ways to style your pages. In addition to using external style sheets, you can apply inline or internal styles directly in your HTML document.

### Inline Style:
Inline styling means that you are specifying styles directly within HTML elements using the style attribute. Here is an example:

```
<p style="color: blue; font-size: 18px;">This paragraph has an inline style.</p>
```

In the example above, the style attribute in the <p> element contains the directly specified style rules. You can define several CSS properties separated by semicolons.

Using inline styling is useful when you want to apply specific styles to only a particular element and don't want to create separate style rules or edit external style sheets.

### Internal Style:
Internal styling means that you are defining style rules within the header of your HTML document using the <style> element. Here is an example:

```
<!DOCTYPE html>
<html>
<head>
  <style>
    p {
      color: blue;
      font-size: 18px;
    }
  </style>
</head>
<body>
  <p>This paragraph has an internal style.</p>
</body>
</html>
```

In the example above, the <style> element within the header contains the style rules that will be applied to all <p> elements in the HTML page. You can define style rules using common CSS selectors and desired properties.

Internal styling is useful when you want to apply styles to a specific set of elements within an HTML page without having to create a separate external style sheet.

However, it's a good practice to use external style sheets to apply styles globally, so you keep your HTML clean and separate from the presentation.

## CSS selectors

CSS selectors are used to select HTML elements to apply styling rules to. There are several types of selectors available in CSS that allow you to locate specific elements based on their characteristics or relationships with other elements. Here are some common examples of CSS selectors:

**Item selector**: Select all items matching a certain item name. For example:

```
p {
  color: blue;
}
```

**Class selector**: Select elements that have the corresponding class attribute. For example:

```
.my style {
  font-size: 18px;
}
```

**ID selector**: Select the element with the corresponding id attribute. For example:

```
#my-item {
  background-color: yellow;
}
```

**Descending selector**: Select child elements of a specific element. For example:

```
div p {
  font-weight: bold;
}
```

**Direct child selector**: Select direct child elements of a specific element. For example:

```
ul > li {
  color: red;
}
```

**Attribute selector**: Select elements that have a specific attribute or an attribute with a specific value. For example:

```
input[type="text"] {
  border: 1px solid black;
}
```

These are just a few examples of CSS selectors, but there are many others that allow for more precise selection of HTML elements. By using CSS selectors appropriately, you can apply specific style rules to the desired elements in your HTML page.

## Common Formatting Properties

There are many common formatting properties in CSS that allow you to control the look and layout of HTML elements. Here are some of the more common formatting properties:

- **color**: Specifies the color of the text.

- **font-family**: Specifies the font to use for the text.

- **font-size**: Specifies the font size.

- **font-weight**: Specifies the font weight (for example, regular, bold).

- **text-align**: Specifies text alignment (for example, left, right, center).

- **text-decoration**: Specifies the text decoration (for example, underline, strikethrough).

- **background-color**: Specifies the background color of the item.

- **padding**: Specifies the internal space between an element's content and its borders.

- **margin**: Specifies the outer space around an element.

- **border**: Specifies the style, thickness, and color of an element's border.

- **width**: Specifies the width of an element.

- **height**: Specifies the height of an element.

- **display**: Specifies the display type of an element (for example, block, inline, inline-block).

- **position**: Specifies the type of placement of an element (for example, static, relative, absolute).

- **float**: Specifies the lateral alignment of an element with respect to its parent elements.

These are just some of the common formatting properties in CSS. There are many others that allow you to control specific details of the appearance and layout of HTML elements. Using these properties in combination with CSS selectors, you can create your own styles and adapt the page design to your needs.

## Layout with Div And Float

Divs are block elements that are often used as containers to group and organize other elements. They can be used to create flexible and complex layouts. In combination with the float CSS property, you can position divs to achieve a desired layout.

Below is an example of how you can use divs and floats to create a layout.

**HTML structure**:
Start by building the basic structure of your layout using divs. For example:

```
<div class="container">
 <div class="sidebar">
  <!-- Sidebar content -->
 </div>
 <div class="main-content">
  <!-- Main content -->
 </div>
</div>
```

In this example, we have a main div with the "container" class that contains two internal divs: one with the "sidebar" class and the other with the "main-content" class. This is just a simple example structure, you can modify it according to your needs.

**CSS float**:
To position divs within the layout, you can use the float CSS property. For example:

```
.sidebar {
 float: left;
 width: 25%;
}

.main-content {
 float: right;
 width: 75%;
}
```

In this example, the sidebar is positioned to the left using float: left, while the main content is positioned to the right using float: right. The specified widths ensure that the sidebar takes up 25% of the total width and the main content takes up 75%. You can adjust the widths according to your preferences.

**Cleaning the float**:
When using floats, you may run into a problem known as "float clearing" or "clearfix". To make sure the layout works correctly, you may need to do a cleanup of the float. There are several techniques for doing this, but one of the most common is to apply the CSS property clear: both to an element following the float divs. For example:

```
<div class="container">
 <div class="sidebar">
  <!-- Sidebar content -->
 </div>
 <div class="main-content">
```

```
    <!-- Main content -->
  </div>
  <div class="clearfix"></div>
</div>
```

```
.clearfix {
  clear: both;
}
```

In this example, a div with the "clearfix" class is added to the end of the main div to clean up the float.

## Media Query for Responsiveness

Media queries are a vital tool for creating responsive design in HTML and CSS. Let you apply different styles based on screen size or other device characteristics.

Here's how to use media queries to make your website responsive:

**Definition of a media query**:
A media query is defined within a CSS style block using the @media at-rule. For example:

```
@media (max-width: 768px) {
  /* Styles to apply when max screen width is 768px */
}
```

In this example, the CSS codes inside the curly braces will only be applied when the maximum screen width is 768 pixels or less.

**Specify the characteristics of the device**:
You can specify various device characteristics, such as screen width, screen height, orientation, and more. For example:

```
@media (min-width: 768px) and (max-width: 1024px) {
  /* Styles to apply when screen width is between 768px and 1024px */
}
```

In this case, the CSS codes inside the curly braces will only be applied when the screen width is between 768 and 1024 pixels.

**Applying specific styles**:
Within the media query's style block, you can define the style rules you want to apply based on screen size or other characteristics. For example:

```
@media (max-width: 768px) {
```

```
body {
  font-size: 14px;
}
.container {
  width: 90%;
}
}
```

In this example, the text will have a font size of 14 pixels and the container will have a width of 90% when the screen width is 768 pixels or less.

Using media queries, you can adjust your website design to different screen sizes and provide an optimal user experience on devices of various sizes.

# Advanced Elements

## Frame and Iframe

Frames and iframes are HTML elements used to create and embed multiple content within a web page. However, frames are considered obsolete in HTML5, while iframes are still widely used.

**Frame**:
Frames allow you to divide your browser window into multiple sections, each of which can display a separate HTML document. However, frames have some usability and accessibility issues, which is why they are not recommended in HTML5. The HTML element for frames is **\<frame\>**, and is usually used inside a \<frameset\> element to define the frame structure. For example:

```
<!DOCTYPE html>
<html>
 <head>
  <title>Document title</title>
 </head>
 <frameset cols="25%,75%">
  <frame src="frame1.html">
  <frame src="frame2.html">
 </frameset>
</html>
```

**Iframe**:
Iframes allow you to embed an HTML page within another HTML page. This can be useful for embedding third-party content such as videos, maps or widgets within a web page. The HTML element for iframes is **\<iframe\>**, and is used when specifying the URL of the document you want to embed. For example:

```
<!DOCTYPE html>
<html>
 <head>
  <title>Document title</title>
 </head>
 <body>
  <h1>My web page</h1>
  <iframe src="https://www.example.com"></iframe>
 </body>
</html>
```

Iframes offer more flexibility than frames, allowing you to embed content from external sources. However, it is important to pay attention to the source of embedded content, as it may present security risks or performance issues.

In general, it's best to avoid using frames and instead use iframes, when needed, to more securely and flexibly embed external content.

# HTML5 semantic elements

HTML5 introduces a number of new semantic elements that allow you to structure and describe the content of a web page in a more meaningful way. These semantic elements were introduced to improve accessibility, indexing by search engines, and understanding of the content by developers and browsers. Here are some examples of HTML5 semantic elements:

- **header**: Represents the header of a section or document and can contain elements such as the page title, logo or main navigation menu.

- **are not**: Defines a navigation section, such as a navigation menu containing links to different pages or sections of the site.

- **section**: Indicates a thematic section within a document. It can be used to group and identify related content, such as articles or blocks of text.

- **article**: Represents a self-contained unit of content, such as a news article, blog post, or comment. It must make self-contained sense and can be distributed or reused separately.

- **aside**: Indicates content that is related to surrounding content, but can be considered separate from it. It usually contains additional information, such as notes, references or advertisements.

- **main**: Defines the main content of a page, excluding the header, footer and side sections. It is recommended that you use the main element only once in a document.

- **footer**: Represents the footer of a section or document and can contain information such as contact details, links to related pages or the author of the content.

- **figure** and **figcaption**: The figure element is used to represent multimedia content, such as images or videos, along with their title or description using the figcaption element.

- **time**: Used to represent a date or time. It can be useful to indicate the publication date of an article or the time of an event.

These are just a few examples of HTML5 semantic elements. By using these semantic elements correctly, it is possible to create a clearer and more meaningful structure for the content of a web page, improving the accessibility and understanding of the document by browsers and users.

It is important to note that HTML5 semantic elements can be used in conjunction with class and id attributes to provide additional information about the purpose and meaning of the content.

## Canvas and HTML5 Graphics

HTML5 offers an element called <canvas> that allows you to create dynamic graphics within a web page using JavaScript. The canvas provides a drawing area on which you can draw shapes, lines, text, images, and even animations.

**Creation of the canvas**: You can insert a canvas into your HTML page using the <canvas> tag. You must also specify the width and height of the canvas using the width and height attributes. For example:

```
<canvas id="myCanvas" width="500" height="300"></canvas>
```

**Context recovery**: In order to draw on the canvas, you need to retrieve the graphic context using JavaScript. You can do this using the getContext() method on the canvas. For example:

```
var canvas = document.getElementById("myCanvas");
var context = canvas.getContext("2d");
```

**Drawing of elements**: Once you have the context, you can use a variety of methods to draw elements on the canvas. Some of the common methods include:

- **context.fillRect(x, y, width, height)**: Draw a filled rectangle at the specified coordinates.

- **context.strokeRect(x, y, width, height)**: Draws a rectangle only with outlines at the specified coordinates.

- **context.beginPath(), context.lineTo(x, y), context.stroke()**: Draw a line from the specified points.

- **context.arc(x, y, radius, startAngle, endAngle), context.fill()**: Draw an arc or circle at the specified coordinates.

**Color manipulation**: You can customize the colors using the context's fillStyle and strokeStyle attributes. For example, you can set the fill color using the following code:

```
context.fillStyle = "red";
```

**Animation management**: Using the canvas and JavaScript, you can create dynamic animations. You can use the feature**requestAnimationFrame()** to run a smooth animation in the browser.

# Optimization and Best Practices

## Structure and Organization of the Code

The structure and organization of HTML code is important in making your code readable, maintainable, and understandable. Here are some tips for effectively organizing your HTML code:

- **Use a tree structure**: HTML follows a hierarchical tree structure. Make sure you organize your elements hierarchically and use opening and closing tags properly to delimit different levels of content. This will make your code clearer and easier to read.

- **Indentation**: Use indentation to highlight the hierarchical structure of your code. Indent nested code blocks using spaces or tabs to improve readability.

- **Comments**: Use comments to describe the meaning or function of certain sections of your code. Comments also help other people understand your code and make future maintenance easier. You can use the <!-- --> tag to insert comments in your HTML code.

- **Divide the code into sections**: If your HTML document is very long or complex, consider dividing it into logical sections. You can use HTML5 semantic elements like <header>, <footer>, <nav>, <section>, <article>, etc., to identify and separate different parts of your document.

- **Meaningful class names and IDs**: Assign meaningful class names and IDs to HTML elements to make them easier to identify and manipulate through CSS and JavaScript. Use class names and IDs that describe the element's role or function in the context of your page.

- **Outsource CSS and scripts**: Whenever possible, separate your CSS and JavaScript code into external files and link them to your HTML document using <link> and <script> tags. This improves the readability of your HTML code and makes maintenance easier.

- **Use significant indentation in CSS**: If you're using CSS, make sure you significantly indent your CSS rules to highlight the structure of your selectors and declarations.

- **Validate your code**: Use HTML validation tools to make sure your code compiles with HTML standards. This will help you spot syntax errors and ensure proper structure of your code.

By following these code organization practices, you'll make your HTML more clean, readable, and maintainable.

## Image Optimization

Image optimization is an important practice to make sure that images load quickly and don't clutter web pages too much.

- **Compress images**: Reduce the file size of images using compression. You can use online image compression tools or image editing software to save images with optimized quality.

- **Use the right formats**: Choose the most suitable image format for your needs. For example, photographic images usually work best with formats like JPEG, while images with transparency can be saved as PNG. Avoid using the uncompressed BMP format.

- **Resize images**: Reduce the physical size of images to the actual size they will be displayed on your website. Do not upload images larger than necessary.

- **Use the srcset tag**: Use the srcset tag to provide different versions of the image based on screen size. This way, browsers can automatically choose the most suitable version of the image for the device in use.

- **Lazy loading**: Implement lazy loading to load images only when they become visible within the browser window. This can greatly improve page load times, especially for pages with lots of images.

- **Use CDNs**: Consider using a Content Delivery Network (CDN) to host your images. CDNs offer a server infrastructure that is distributed around the world, allowing images to load faster by having servers close to users.

- **Image cache**: Configure the image cache in your web server so that images are cached in users' browsers for a specified period of time. This way, images can load faster when a user visits multiple pages on your site.

- **Tests and measurements**: Use web performance testing tools to evaluate your site's performance, including image loading. You can use tools like Google PageSpeed Insights or GTmetrix to get specific image optimization recommendations.

Image optimization is a vital step in ensuring a positive user experience and improving the overall performance of your website. Make sure you adopt these practices to reduce the size of your images and improve loading times.

## Accessibility and SEO

Both accessibility and search engine optimization (SEO) are important to ensure that your website is accessible to all users and that it is properly detected and indexed by search engines. By following these guidelines, you can improve user experience and increase the visibility of your website online.

**Accessibility**:

- **Use a semantic structure**: Correctly use HTML5 semantic elements like <header>, <nav>, <main>, <section>, <article>, etc. These elements provide clear context and structure for screen readers and other assistance tools.

- **Provide alt text for images**: Use the alt attribute to provide a text description of the images. This allows visually impaired users or those using screen readers to understand the content of the image.

- **Use descriptive links**: Make sure your links have meaningful descriptive text. Avoid using links like "click here" or "read more", but rather use text that clearly describes the destination of the link.

- **Color contrast:** Make sure there is adequate contrast between the text and the background to improve readability. Avoid color combinations that may be difficult for people with vision impairment or vision impairment to read.

- **Logical reading order**: Make sure the reading order of your website content is logical and consistent, even without the use of visual styling. This is especially important for users using screen readers or alternative navigation devices.

**SEO (Search Engine Optimization)**:

- **Use appropriate header tags**: Use <h1> - <h6> header tags correctly to structure your page. Make sure the <h1> tag contains the main title of the page and use subsequent header tags for subheadings and sections.

- **Use meta tags**: Include relevant meta tags such as the page title (<title>) and a description of the content (<meta name="description" content="...">). These elements can help search engines understand your content and show meaningful thumbnails in search results.

- **Readable URLs**: Use readable and descriptive URLs that reflect the content of the page. Avoid URLs that are too long or have complex parameters.

- **Use emphasized text tags**: Use <strong> and <em> tags to emphasize important keywords or phrases in your content. This can help search engines identify the highlights of your page.

- **Link structure**: Make sure your links have a clear and meaningful structure. Use descriptive texts and link to related pages appropriately. This can help build a solid link architecture for your website.

## Validation of the HTML Code

HTML code validation is a process that consists of verifying that your HTML code conforms to the standards set by the W3C (World Wide Web Consortium). Validating HTML code can help you spot any errors or problems in your code and ensure that your website is structured correctly.

There are several online tools you can use to validate your HTML code. One of the most common is the W3C HTML validator, which you can find at the web address "https://validator.w3.org/". To validate your HTML code, you can simply paste the code into the input field and start the validation. The validator will give you a detailed report of any errors or warnings that may be present in your code.

Validating HTML code is important for several reasons:

- **Code correctness**: HTML code validation helps you identify and fix any errors in your code. This ensures that your website displays correctly on different browsers and devices.

- **Accessibility**: Valid HTML code helps make your website more accessible to all users, including those with disabilities or using assistive technologies such as screen readers.

- **Future compatibility**: HTML code validation helps you write code that conforms to current web standards. This means that your website will be more compatible with future versions of HTML and will benefit from new features and improvements.

- **Performance improvement:** Good and well-structured HTML code can help improve the overall performance of your website. This can translate into faster loading times and a better user experience.

Remember that validating HTML code is a continuous process. You should always try to write clean and valid code, and validate your work regularly while developing your website.

## Test and Debug

In the process of developing a website in HTML, it is vital to test and fix any bugs or debugging issues to ensure that the site works well on different browsers and devices. Here are some tips for testing and debugging HTML code:

- **Code validation**: As mentioned earlier, use validation tools such as the W3C HTML Validator to verify that your HTML code conforms to standards. This will help you locate and fix errors in your code.

- **Test on different browsers**: Check that your website works on different browsers, such as Google Chrome, Mozilla Firefox, Safari, Internet Explorer, etc. Each browser may interpret HTML code slightly differently, so it's important to check compatibility and troubleshoot any browser-specific issues.

- **Test on different devices**: Make sure your website is responsive and works well on different devices, such as desktop, tablet and mobile. Use responsive development tools or test your website on real devices to see how it looks and behaves on different screen sizes.

- **Developer Console**: Use your browser's built-in developer console to check for any scripting errors, warnings, or debugging messages. You can bring up the developer console by pressing the F12 key in most browsers.

- **Debugging tools**: There are several debugging tools available, such as Firebug for Firefox or Google Chrome Developer Tools, which offer advanced debugging, element inspection, network request tracing, and more. These tools can help you find and fix specific problems in your HTML code.

- **Workflow testing**: Make sure you also test the workflow and interactive features of your website, such as form submission, page navigation, error handling, etc. Verify that all connections and interactions are working properly.

- **Regular updates:** Keep your website up-to-date, both code-wise and feature-wise. Test and debug regularly even after you make changes or updates to your site.

Testing and debugging are iterative processes that require patience and attention to detail. It is important to troubleshoot and optimize your HTML code to ensure a good user experience and smooth running of your website.

# Advanced CSS

## Pseudoclasses and Pseudoelements

In CSS, pseudoclasses and pseudoelements are used to select and style specific parts of HTML elements according to different states or positions. These allow you to apply additional styles to specific elements without having to edit the HTML markup directly.

Pseudoclasses are used to select elements based on a particular state or user interaction. For example, the :hover pseudo-class can be used to apply a style when the mouse cursor is over an element. Other common pseudoclasses include :active for an element's active state (when pressed), :focus for the element currently in focus, and :visited for visited links.

Here's an example of using the :hover pseudo-class to change the background color of an element when the mouse cursor hovers over it:

```
a:hover {
  background-color: yellow;
}
```

Pseudo-elements, on the other hand, are used to select and style specific parts of an element. They are represented with a double colon:: to distinguish them from pseudoclasses. For example, the ::before pseudo-element can be used to insert content before the selected element, while the ::after pseudo-element can be used to insert content after the selected element.

Here's an example of using the ::before pseudo-element to insert an icon before the text of an element:

```
p::before {
  content: "\f105"; /* Unicode code of the icon */
  font-family: "Font Awesome"; /* Font that contains the icon */
  margin-right: 5px;
}
```

Pseudoclasses and pseudoelements provide greater flexibility in selecting and stylizing HTML elements. They allow you to apply specific styles to certain situations or parts of elements without having to add classes or change HTML markup.

## Box Model and Margins

The Box Model is a fundamental concept in CSS that defines the structure and behavior of an HTML element. Each HTML element is represented as a rectangular "box", which includes four main components: the content, the padding, the border and the margins.

- **Content**: The content represents the internal area of the box that contains the text, images or other elements within the HTML element.

- **Padding**: The padding is the transparent space that surrounds the content inside the box. It can be set using the CSS property padding and can have different values for top, right, bottom and left padding.

- **Edge**: The border is a line that surrounds the padding and the contents of the box. It can be set using the CSS border property and can have different styles, weights and colors.

- **Margins**: Margins represent the empty space outside the box, which separates the element from other surrounding elements. It can be set using the CSS margin property and can have different values for top, right, bottom and left margin.

Here is an example of how the different components of the Box Model are displayed:

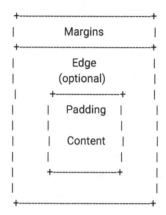

Margins are important because they determine the space between an element and other surrounding elements. For example, if you apply a bottom margin to an element, this will create a gap between the element and the underlying element.

You can control the Box Model using different CSS properties like width and height for the content, padding for the padding, border for the border and margin for the margins. It is important to consider the Box Model when designing and developing a web page, as it affects the arrangement and spacing of elements.

You can also use the box-sizing and margin-collapse properties to control the behavior of the Box Model more precisely and handle any inconsistencies between browsers.


## Positioning and Z-index

Positioning and z-index are two important concepts for controlling the position of HTML elements in a web page.

Positioning determines how an element is positioned within the document flow and can be managed using the following CSS properties:

- **static** (default): The item is placed in the normal flow of the document. It is not possible to change the default placement using other properties.

- **relative**: The item is moved from its normal position. You can use the top, right, bottom and left properties to specify the offset from its normal placement.

- **absolute**: The element is positioned based on the position of its parent element which has relative or absolute positioning. It can be moved using the top, right, bottom and left properties. Elements with absolute positioning are removed from the normal flow of the document.

- **fixed**: The element is positioned according to the browser viewing window, remaining fixed even when scrolling. It can be moved using the top, right, bottom and left properties. Elements with fixed placement are removed from the normal flow of the document.

- **sticky**: The item is positioned based on its normal position until the viewing window reaches a specific position, after which it becomes sticky positioned relative to that position.

The property **z-index** it is used to manage the overlapping of elements based on their numerical value. A higher z-index value means that the element will appear above elements with a lower z-index value. However, the z-index only affects elements that have non-static positioning (such as relative, absolute, or fixed).

Here is an example of using positioning and z-index:

```
div {
  position: relative;
  top: 20px;
  left: 30px;
  z-index: 2;
}

p {
  position: absolute;
  top: 50px;
  left: 50px;
  z-index: 1;
}
```

In this example, the div element will have relative positioning and will be moved 20px down and 30px to the left from its normal position. Also, it will have a z-index of 2, so it will display above the p element which has a z-index of 1.


## Animations and Transitions

Animations and transitions allow you to add dynamism and interactivity to web pages. They allow you to create visual effects, smooth transitions between element states, and custom animations.

Animations in HTML and CSS can be made using a variety of techniques, including:

- **CSS transitions**: CSS transitions allow you to animate the style properties of an element smoothly and gradually. You can specify the duration, transition type, and other options to create transition effects between states of an item. For example, you can animate an element's background color, size, or position during a state change.

- **CSS animations**: CSS animations offer more control and flexibility than transitions. They allow you to define keyframes that specify the different stages of the animation and the properties that should change in each frame. You can define the duration, type of animation, number of repetitions and other options to create complex and customized animations.

- **JavaScript libraries**: There are a number of JavaScript libraries, such as jQuery, GSAP (GreenSock Animation Platform), and Anime.js, that make it easy to create rich animations. These libraries offer more advanced features, such as animating multiple elements simultaneously, precise timing control, and special effects.

Using animations and transitions can improve user experience and make web pages more appealing. However, it's important to use them sparingly and take performance and accessibility into account. Here are some tips for using animations correctly:

- Limit the use of heavy or overly complex animations, so as not to clog the pages loading.

- Make sure that animations do not interfere with the usability of the content and do not cause confusion or disorientation for the user.

- Use subtle and elegant animations to improve the readability and usability of the website, such as smooth transitions between pages or feedback effects on user interaction.

- Test animations on different devices and browsers to ensure proper display and a consistent experience.

In conclusion, animations and transitions are powerful tools for enhancing the look and interactivity of web pages. With the right amount of creativity and a focus on performance, engaging and engaging experiences for users can be created.


## Responsive Design with CSS Grid and Flexbox

Responsive design is a web design and development methodology that focuses on creating websites that adapt and respond optimally to different devices and screen sizes, providing a good user experience on desktop, tablet and mobile devices.

**CSS Grid**: CSS Grid Layout is a CSS module that allows you to create complex and flexible page layouts. It consists of a two-dimensional grid system, where rows and columns can be defined to place items within a grid. With CSS Grid, you can precisely control the position and size of elements on the page. It's especially useful for creating grid layouts, such as image grids or sections of content.

**Flexbox**: Flexbox, short for Flexible Box Layout, is a CSS module that offers a flexible and dynamic layout system. It allows you to arrange the items inside a container in one direction (horizontal or vertical) and manage their automatic resizing to fit the available space. Flexbox is particularly suitable for creating one-dimensional layouts, such as menus, navigation bars and item lists.

Both CSS Grid and Flexbox are supported by all major modern browsers and offer a wide range of features for creating responsive layouts. Here are some of their key features:

**CSS Grid:**

- Flexible row and column definition to create complex layouts.

- Precise positioning of items within the grid using cell coordinates.

- Support for creating responsive layouts using media queries and cell size changes.

- Create grid layouts with flexible spacing and alignment of elements.

**Flexbox:**

- Arranging elements in a main direction (row or column).

- Control the automatic resizing of items to fit the available space.

- Flexible alignment of elements along the main and cross axis.

- Item flow management, including managing the reordering of items across different devices.

The combination of CSS Grid and Flexbox offers great flexibility in creating responsive and adaptable layouts. You can use both methods in combination to get the most control over the placement of elements on the page. Additionally, they can be used in conjunction with other responsive design techniques, such as using media queries to adjust the layout based on screen size.
Remember that choosing between CSS Grid and Flexbox depends on the type of layout you want to create. Flexbox is ideal for one-dimensional layouts, while CSS Grid is more suitable for two-dimensional and complex layouts. You can experiment and combine both methods to get the best results for your responsive design project.

Here are some examples of how to use CSS Grid and Flexbox to create responsive layouts:

**Responsive grid layout with CSS Grid**

```
<div class="grid-container">
  <div class="item">Item 1</div>
  <div class="item">Item 2</div>
  <div class="item">Item 3</div>
</div>
```

```
.grid-container {
  display: grid;
  grid-template-columns: 1fr 1fr 1fr;
  grid-gap: 10px;
}

.item {
```

```
    background-color: #ccc;
    padding: 10px;
}
```

In this example, we're using CSS Grid to create a grid layout with three equal columns. Divs with class "item" represent the items within the grid. Using the grid-template-columns and grid-gap properties, we define the desired number of columns and the space between cells. The grid will automatically adjust based on the width of the parent container.

**Layout responsive with Flexbox**

```
<div class="flex-container">
  <div class="item">Item 1</div>
  <div class="item">Item 2</div>
  <div class="item">Item 3</div>
</div>
```

```
.flex-container {
  display: flex;
  flex-wrap: wrap;
  justify-content: space-between;
}

.item {
  flex-basis: 30%;
  background-color: #ccc;
  padding: 10px;
  margin-bottom: 10px;
}
```

In this example, we're using Flexbox to create a responsive layout with three elements inside a flex container. We use the flex-wrap property to make elements wrap across multiple lines when space is limited. The justify-content: space-between property distributes elements evenly along the main axis, creating space between them. With flex-basis, we set the basic width of the elements to 30% to fit the desired layout.

## JavaScript and Dynamic Interaction

### Introduction to JavaScript

JavaScript is an interpreted programming language used primarily to add interactivity and dynamism to web pages. It is one of the three basic pillars of web development along with HTML and CSS. While HTML deals with the structure of the content and CSS deals with the visual presentation, JavaScript is responsible for the interaction and logic of page behavior.

### Embed JavaScript in HTML

To embed JavaScript in an HTML document, you can use the <script> tag. Here are three common ways to do this.

**Script inline**: You can place JavaScript code directly inside the <script> tag in the HTML. For example:

```
<!DOCTYPE html>
<html>
<head>
 <title>Document</title>
</head>
<body>
 <h1>Welcome!</h1>

 <script>
  // JavaScript code here
  alert("Hello, world!");
 </script>
</body>
</html>
```

In this example, the JavaScript code is placed directly in the <script> tag. When the page loads, the JavaScript code will be executed.

**External script**: You can link an external JavaScript file using the src attribute of the <script> tag. For example:

```
<!DOCTYPE html>
<html>
<head>
 <title>Document</title>
 <script src="script.js"></script>
</head>
<body>
 <h1>Welcome!</h1>
</body>
```

```
</html>
```

In this case, the external JavaScript file named "script.js" is linked to the HTML page using the src attribute of the <script> tag. Make sure the JavaScript file path is correct and accessible.

**Browser events**: You can bind JavaScript code to browser events using the on attribute on HTML elements. For example:

```
<!DOCTYPE html>
<html>
<head>
  <title>Document</title>
</head>
<body>
  <h1>Welcome!</h1>

  <button onclick="myFunction()">Clicca qui</button>

  <script>
    function myFunction() {
      // JavaScript code here
      alert("You clicked the button!");
    }
  </script>
</body>
</html>
```

In this example, a JavaScript function myFunction() is defined. When the user clicks the button, the function runs and a warning message is displayed.

You can use any of these approaches or a combination of them, depending on the needs of your project. Remember to place the <script> tag inside the <head> tag or <body> tag as needed.


## DOM Manipulation

Manipulating the DOM (Document Object Model) is an essential aspect of JavaScript programming to interact with the elements and content of a web page. The DOM represents the page structure as a tree of objects, allowing you to access, edit, and manipulate HTML elements and their content using JavaScript.

**Select items**: You can select HTML elements using methods like getElementById, getElementsByClassName, getElementsByTagName or querySelector. For example:

```
// Select an item by ID
var myElement = document.getElementById("myElement");

// Select all elements by class
```

```
var elements = document.getElementsByClassName("myClass");

// Select first element for tag
var firstElement = document.getElementsByTagName("p")[0];

// Select the first element that matches the CSS selector
var element = document.querySelector(".mySelector");
```

**Modify the content**: You can change the content of an HTML element using the innerHTML or textContent properties. For example:

```
// Edit the HTML content of an element
myElement.innerHTML = "<strong>Bold text</strong>";

// Edit the text of an element
myElement.textContent = "New text";
```

**Add and delete items:** You can create new HTML elements using the createElement method and add them to the DOM using the appendChild or insertBefore methods. You can also remove items using the removeChild method. For example:

```
// Create a new item
var newElement = document.createElement("div");

// Add the new element as a child of another element
parentElement.appendChild(newElement);

// Insert the new element before another element
parentElement.insertBefore(newElement, existingElement);

// Remove an element from the DOM
parentElement.removeChild(childElement);
```

**Modify attributes**: You can change the attributes of an HTML element using the element's properties. For example:

```
// Modify the "src" attribute of an image
imageElement.src = "new-image.jpg";

// Modify the "class" attribute of an element
element.className = "new-class";

// Modify the "style" attribute of an element
element.style.color = "red";
```

## Events and Event Managers

The purpose of events and event handlers is to create interactivity in web pages. Events are specific actions or situations that occur during a user's interaction with a web page, such as a button click, page load, or mouse movement. Event handlers are the JavaScript functions that execute in response to a certain event.

**Add an event handler**: You can add an event handler to an HTML element using the addEventListener method. This method takes two arguments: the name of the event to listen to and the function to execute when the event occurs. For example, to add an event handler for a button click:

```
var myButton = document.getElementById("myButton");

myButton.addEventListener("click", function() {
  // Code to execute when the button click occurs
});
```

**Remove an event handler**: If you want to remove an event handler from an element, you can use the removeEventListener method. You need to pass the same arguments (event name and event handler function) that you used to add it. For example:

```
myButton.removeEventListener("click", functionName);
```

**Parameter passing**: You can pass additional parameters to the event handler function using an anonymous function or the bind function. For example:

```
myButton.addEventListener("click", function(event) {
  console.log("You clicked the button");
  console.log("Posizione del clic: " + event.clientX + ", " + event.clientY);
});
```

**Common types of events**: There are many event types available, including "click", "mouseover", "keydown", "submit", "load" and many more. You can find a complete list of event types in the JavaScript documentation.

**Events on multiple elements**: You can add event handlers to multiple elements at the same time using loops or methods like querySelectorAll. For example, to add an event handler to all elements with a given class:

```
var elements = document.querySelectorAll(".myClass");

for (var i = 0; i < elements.length; i++) {
  elements[i].addEventListener("click", function() {
    // Code to execute when an element with class "myClass" is clicked
  });
}
```

# Performance Optimization

## Asynchronous Loading of Resources

Asynchronous resource loading is a technique used to improve performance and user experience when loading a web page. It consists of loading the resources independently and asynchronously with respect to the loading of the main HTML document. This allows the browser to continue rendering the page without waiting for the resources to finish loading.

There are several ways to implement asynchronous loading of resources in HTML. Here are some of the most common techniques:

**<script> tag with async attribute**: For asynchronous script loading, you can use the async attribute in the <script> tag. This attribute allows the browser to download and execute the script asynchronously, without interrupting the loading of the HTML document. However, the execution order of scripts can be unpredictable, so make sure the script doesn't depend on external resources or other parts of the HTML document.

```
<script src="script.js" async></script>
```

**<script> tag with the defer attribute**: The defer attribute can be used for asynchronous loading of scripts, but it maintains the execution order of the scripts relative to their declaration order in the HTML document. Scripts with the defer attribute are executed only after the HTML document has been fully parsed. This is especially useful when the script depends on the full DOM tree or other resources loaded into the document.

```
<script src="script.js" defer></script>
```

**Asynchronous loading of external resources**: For asynchronous loading of external resources such as CSS stylesheets or images, you can use JavaScript to create the appropriate elements (for example, <link> tags for CSS or <img> tags for images) and dynamically add them to the document. In this way, the loading of resources can happen asynchronously with respect to the loading of the main HTML document.

```
<script>
  var link = document.createElement('link');
  link.rel = 'stylesheet';
  link.href = 'style.css';
  document.head.appendChild(link);
</script>
```

**Using libraries or frameworks**: There are also libraries or frameworks, such as RequireJS or Webpack, that offer advanced capabilities for asynchronous resource loading. These libraries provide more advanced resource loading and dependency management, further improving loading performance.

Keep in mind that asynchronous resource loading may involve some additional considerations, such as managing dependencies between resources and script execution order. Make sure you test your code carefully to ensure that everything works correctly and that there are no dependency errors or conflicts.

## Code Compression and Minification

HTML code compression and minification are techniques used to reduce the size of HTML files sent to the browser, thereby improving website performance. These techniques reduce page load time, reduce bandwidth usage, and improve the overall user experience.

- **Compression**: HTML code compression is about reducing the size of the HTML file by removing whitespace, comments, and other unnecessary characters. This is accomplished using compression algorithms such as Gzip or Deflate. Compressing HTML code can reduce file size by up to 70-90%, depending on the amount of whitespace and comments in the code.

- **Minification**: Minification of HTML code is a process in which code is minimized in size by removing whitespace, comments and empty lines. Also, HTML element, attribute, and class names are shortened to reduce overall code length. Minification of HTML code can be done manually or through the use of minification tools.

The combined use of compression and minification of HTML code can lead to significant improvements in website performance. By reducing the size of HTML files, page load times are reduced, allowing users to view content faster. Also, reducing the size of HTML files results in lower bandwidth usage, which is especially important for users with slow or limited connections.

To apply HTML code compression and minification, you can use different tools and plugins available online. Some web servers also support HTML file compression natively, so you can enable compression directly on the server.

Remember that while compressing and minifying HTML code can help improve the performance of your website, it's important to test your code carefully after applying these techniques. Make sure your website works properly and that there are no compatibility or rendering issues due to code compression or minification.


## File Caching and Rendering Optimization

File caching and rendering optimization are two important aspects to improve the performance of your HTML website. Both help reduce page load times and optimize the overall user experience.

**File caching**: File caching is a technique which allows files to be temporarily stored on the user's device, so that they can be retrieved quickly without having to request them from the server each time the site is visited. This significantly reduces page load times, as the browser can access cached files directly without having to download them again. To enable file caching, you can use HTTP headers such as "Cache-Control" and "Expires" to specify how long files should be cached in the browser.

**Rendering optimization**: Rendering optimization refers to optimizing the way the browser renders and displays HTML pages. There are several techniques you can use to optimize page rendering:

- **Minimize the use of resources**: Be sure to use web-optimized images and media files to reduce file size and improve loading times. Minimize the use of heavy JavaScript or CSS scripts that may slow down page rendering.

- **Organize HTML code**: Structure your HTML code in a clean and well-organized way, using appropriate semantic elements. This helps the browser better understand the structure and content of the page, improving rendering efficiency.

- **Avoid rendering blocks**: Avoid using render-blocking scripts or styles. This can slow down the loading and display of the main content. Use techniques like asynchronous script injection or CSS code splitting to ensure faster rendering.

- **Optimize CSS and JavaScript**: Minify and unify CSS and JavaScript files, reducing the number of server requests. You can use compression and minification tools to reduce the size of your CSS and JavaScript files.

- **Use pre-rendering techniques**: You can use techniques like prefetching and pre-rendering to anticipate browser requests and prepare pages in advance. This can significantly improve page load times, especially for subsequent links the user may visit.

Implementing these file caching and rendering optimization techniques can go a long way in improving the performance of your HTML website. By reducing page load times and optimizing rendering, you will offer a smoother and faster user experience.

# Security and Best Practices

## Prevention of XSS Attacks

Preventing XSS (Cross-Site Scripting) attacks is a vital practice for ensuring the security of your HTML website. XSS attacks occur when an attacker inserts malicious JavaScript code into user input, which is then executed in the browsers of other users who visit the site.

Here are some practices to prevent XSS attacks in your HTML code:

- **Input validation**: Implements rigorous validation of user input, both client-side and server-side. Make sure that the data entered by users meets certain criteria, such as length, format and the presence of prohibited special characters.

- **Input sanitization**: Use input sanitization features to filter and remove any special characters or malicious JavaScript code. This can be done using HTML escape libraries or functions that convert special characters into HTML entities, thus preventing the code from executing.

- **Data encoding**: When displaying user-entered data on HTML pages, be sure to encode correctly. Use functions like htmlspecialchars to convert special characters into HTML entities, thus preventing the code from being interpreted as markup.

- **Limitation of privileges**: Restrict the privileges of executing JavaScript code within your website. Avoid allowing external JavaScript code or untrusted sources to run.

- **Header HTTP**: Configure HTTP headers correctly to mitigate XSS attacks. Use the Content-Security-Policy header to define the allowed sources for uploading resources and running scripts.

- **Update and patch**: Always keep the frameworks, libraries and software used in your website up to date. Often, developers release security fixes to address known XSS vulnerabilities.

It is important to understand and implement these practices to successfully prevent XSS attacks in your HTML website. Security is a crucial aspect in designing and developing a web application, so take the necessary measures to protect your users and their sensitive data.

## Validation of User Data

Validating user data is an important aspect of creating a secure and functional HTML website. Data validation makes it possible to check that the information entered by users respects certain criteria, such as the correct format, the appropriate length and the presence of allowed characters. This helps ensure that the data you receive is reliable and consistent, reducing the risk of errors or malicious attacks.

Here are some common practices for validating user data in HTML:

- **Client side validation**: You can use HTML input element attributes, such as required, pattern, min, max, maxlength, etc., to define validation requirements directly in the HTML code. For example, you can use the pattern attribute with a regular expression to specify the correct format of an input field.

- **Server side validation**: It is also essential to implement server-side data validation to ensure greater security. While client-side validation can be useful for providing instant feedback to the user, it can be easily circumvented. Server-side validation, on the other hand, offers greater protection, as the data is also checked after it is sent to the server.

- **Use of validation libraries**: You can use JavaScript libraries, such as jQuery Validation, Parsley.js or validate.js, which simplify the implementation of user data validation. These libraries offer advanced features, such as custom validation, error handling, and display of validation messages.

- **Custom validation**: If the validation requirements cannot be met using the predefined HTML attributes, you can implement your own custom validation logic using JavaScript. You can define validation functions that check the data entered by users and return a boolean value to indicate whether the data is valid or not.

- **Error display**: It is important to provide clear feedback to users when their data fails validation. You can use custom error messages or CSS styles to highlight invalid input fields and provide instructions about the mistake.

## Protection Against CSRF Attacks

Protection against cross-site request forgery (CSRF) attacks is critical to ensuring the security of HTML web applications. CSRF is a type of attack in which an attacker exploits the trust of a legitimate user to perform unauthorized actions without their knowledge.

Here are some common techniques to protect your HTML applications from CSRF attacks:

- **Using CSRF Tokens**: One of the most effective techniques to protect against CSRF attacks is the use of CSRF tokens. These tokens are generated by the server and included in requests that change the state of the application (for example, POST, PUT, DELETE requests). The server verifies that the token sent in the request matches the one previously generated, thus blocking unauthorized CSRF requests.

- **Action confirmation**: For actions that may have significant consequences, such as deleting data or changing account settings, you can request explicit confirmation from the user before performing the action. This may include the use of confirmation dialogs or requests for confirmation through a separate page.

- **Restricting access via the header referer**: The Referer header contains the URL of the page that made the request. You can configure the server to verify that the Referer header matches the URL of the application, in order to limit requests from other sources.

- **Setting SameSite flags**: You can set the SameSite attribute on cookies to specify that they should only be sent when the request comes from the same site. This helps prevent the use of cookies in CSRF requests from external sites.

- **Using session tokens**: Along with CSRF tokens, it is also important to use session tokens to authenticate users and verify authorization for requests. Session tokens must be managed properly and expire after a certain period of inactivity.

- **Implementation of security controls**: It is imperative that you implement proper security controls at the server configuration and code level. These may include properly configuring cross-origin resource sharing (CORS) policies, validating input data, protecting against scripting attacks, and using secure libraries or frameworks.

## SSL and HTTPS for Communications Security

SSL (Secure Sockets Layer) and HTTPS (Hypertext Transfer Protocol Secure) are cryptographic protocols used to ensure the security of communications on the Internet.

SSL is a protocol that establishes an encrypted connection between a client and a server. This protocol protects the data exchanged between the client and the server from any attempts of interception or manipulation by third parties.

HTTPS, on the other hand, is a secure version of the HTTP protocol that uses SSL to encrypt the communication between the client and the server. When a website uses HTTPS, a secure connection is established and a green padlock appears in the browser's address bar to indicate that the connection is secure.

Using SSL and HTTPS offers several advantages in terms of communication security:

- **Data encryption**: SSL encrypts the data transmitted between the client and the server, making it unreadable for any intruders attempting to intercept the communication. This protects sensitive information, such as user passwords or payment details, during the transfer.

- **Server authentication**: SSL authenticates the server's identity, ensuring that the client is connecting to the desired website and not a spoofed or compromised website. This helps prevent phishing attacks and ensures user trust in the website.

- **Data Integrity**: SSL also includes mechanisms for verifying the integrity of transmitted data. This means that the data cannot be altered or manipulated during transmission. If the data changes during the transfer, the connection is terminated to ensure user safety.

- **Ranking SEO**: Search engines like Google favor websites using HTTPS in search result rankings. Therefore, adopting HTTPS can improve your website's visibility and online reputation.

To implement SSL and HTTPS on your HTML website, you need to obtain an SSL certificate from a trusted certificate authority and correctly configure your web server to use the certificate. There are several SSL certificate options available, including paid certificates and free certificates like Let's Encrypt.

# Conclusions and insights

## Summary of Key Concepts

HTML (HyperText Markup Language) is the standard markup language for creating web pages. Some key concepts of HTML include:

- **Structure**: HTML defines the structure of a web page using elements such as <html>, <head> and <body>. These elements provide the basic structure of the HTML document.

- **Tag** and **elements**: HTML uses tags to define page elements. For example, <p> is used for paragraphs, <h1> - <h6> for headings, <a> for hyperlinks, and so on.

- **Attributes**: Attributes provide more information about HTML elements. For example, the "src" attribute is used to specify the URL of an image in the <img> tag, while the "href" attribute is used to define the destination link in the <a> tag.

- **Heading** and **body**: The header (<head>) contains the header information of the document, such as the page title and links to external style sheets, while the body (<body>) contains the actual content of the page.

- **Link** and **connections**: HTML allows you to create hyperlinks using the <a> tag. These links can point to external web pages, sections of the same page or email addresses.

- **Images** and **media**: HTML allows you to embed images and media in web pages by using the <img> tag for images and tags such as <audio> and <video> for audio and video.

- **Form** and **input**: HTML offers the possibility to create forms using the <form> tag. Input fields such as text boxes, checkboxes, radio buttons and drop down menus can be used to collect data from users.

- **Style** and **presentation**: HTML is used to define the structure of the contents, while CSS (Cascading Style Sheets) is used to define the style and presentation of the HTML elements.

- **Interactivity with JavaScript**: HTML can be made interactive using JavaScript. JavaScript can be embedded directly into HTML pages or included in external files.

- **Compatibility** and **standardization**: HTML is supported by all modern web browsers and is a standardized language with specifications defined by the W3C (World Wide Web Consortium).

## Exercise Projects

Here are some tutorial projects you can make using HTML:

- **Personal page**: Create a web page that serves as your personal presentation. Include information about yourself, your skills, your interests and maybe even your CV.

- **Travel site**: Build a website featuring different travel destinations. Include pictures, descriptions and useful information about each destination.

- **Photo gallery**: Create an online photo gallery where you can showcase your favorite photos. Organize photos into different categories or albums.

- **Personal blog**: Build a personal blog where you can post articles on topics that interest you. Also include a comment form for readers to interact with you.

- **Restaurant site**: Create a website for an imaginary or real restaurant. Include information about the menu, opening hours, location and reservations.

- **Portfolio of projects**: Create an online portfolio to showcase your past projects and work. Include descriptions, images, and links to the projects themselves.

- **News site**: Create a website that features the latest news on a certain topic. Organize the news by categories and allow users to comment on the articles.

- **Music site**: Build a dedicated music website, where you can share your favorite songs, create playlists, and provide information about artists and albums.

These practice projects allow you to apply your knowledge of HTML in creative and practical ways. Experiment with the features of HTML and try to improve your web page creation skills. Good fun!

## Additional Learning Resources

Remember that practice is key to learning HTML. If you'd like to further your HTML knowledge, here are some learning resources you might find helpful:

- **Official documentation**: The W3C (World Wide Web Consortium) provides comprehensive documentation on HTML on its website. You can consult the official HTML specification to fully understand the language and its more advanced features.

- **Mozilla Developer Network (MDN)**: MDN offers a complete guide to HTML with examples, tutorials and references. It's a reliable resource for learning HTML and keeping up with the latest news.

- **Books**: Consult the various books in the series **Easy Code** to broaden your knowledge.

- **Forums and online communities**: Participating in discussion forums and online communities dedicated to web development allows you to connect with other enthusiasts and share your experiences. You can ask questions, get advice and exchange valuable information.

## Outro

And with this our adventure in the fascinating world of HTML concludes. We hope that, as promised, "Easy HTML - Handy Guide" has provided you with the solid foundation and tools necessary to create stunning and engaging web pages.

Through these pages, we have explored the universe of HTML, revealing its secrets and learning to master its powerful tools. We've discovered how to structure your code, create interactive elements, bring your ideas to life with style and design, and so much more.

But remember, the beauty of HTML lies in its versatility. Now that you've learned the basics, you're free to explore further frontiers, experiment with new language features, and challenge your creativity.

Be bold, be innovative, and don't be afraid to test your skills. With "Easy HTML - Handy Guide" in your hands, you are armed with the knowledge that will allow you to create extraordinary web experiences and make your mark in the vast and fascinating online universe.

HTML is constantly evolving and new technologies are constantly emerging. Always be curious, stay up to date with the latest trends and you will continue to grow as a web developer.

Thank you for choosing "Easy HTML - Handy Guide" as your travel companion.

Good luck and happy programming!

www.ingramcontent.com/pod-product-compliance
Lightning Source LLC
LaVergne TN
LVHW081532050326
832903LV00025B/1749